Grade

Classical Guitar Playing

Compiled and edited by
Tony Skinner and Raymond Burley

Printed and bound in Great Britain

Published by Registry Publications

Registry Mews, 11-13 Wilton Rd, Bexhill, Sussex, TN40 1HY

Cover guitars: Rohan Lowe, John Price, Martin Fleeson

A CIP record for this publication is available from the British Library
ISBN: 1-898466-61-0

Compiled for **LCM Exams** by

INTRODUCTION

This publication is part of a progressive series of ten handbooks, primarily intended for candidates considering taking the London College Of Music examinations in classical guitar playing. However, given each handbook's wide content of musical repertoire, and associated educational material, the series provides a solid foundation of musical education for any classical guitar student – whether intending to take an examination or not. Whilst the handbooks can be used for independent study, they are ideally intended as a supplement to individual or group tuition.

Examination entry

An examination entry form is provided at the rear of each handbook. This is the only valid entry form for the London College Of Music classical guitar examinations.

Please note that *if the entry form is detached and lost, it will not be replaced under any circumstances* and the candidate will be required to obtain a replacement handbook to obtain another entry form.

Editorial information

All performance pieces should be played in full, including all repeats shown. The pieces have been edited specifically for examination use, with all non-required repeat markings omitted. Examination performances must be from this handbook edition. Tempos, fingering, and dynamic markings are for general guidance only and need not be rigidly adhered to.

Right-hand fingering is normally shown on the stem side of the notes:
p = thumb; *i* = index; *m* = middle; *a* = third.

Left-hand fingering is shown with the numbers **1 2 3 4**, normally to the left side of the note head.
0 indicates an open string.

String numbers are shown in a circle, normally below the note. For example, ⑥ = 6th string.

Finger shifts are indicated by a small horizontal dash before the left hand finger number.
For example, **2** followed by **-2** indicates that the 2nd finger can stay on the same string but move to another fret as a *guide finger*. The finger shift sign should not be confused with a *slide* or *glissando* (where a longer dash joins two noteheads).

Acknowledgements

The editors acknowledge the help of the many libraries and copyright owners that facilitated access to original manuscripts, source materials and facsimiles during the compilation of this series of books. The editors are grateful for the advice and support of all the members of the Registry Of Guitar Tutors 'Classical Guitar Advisory Panel', and are particularly indebted for the expertise and contributions of:

**Carlos Bonell Hon.RCM, Chris Ackland GRSM LRAM LTCL,
Chaz Hart LRAM, Frank Bliven BM MA, Alan J. Brown LTCL.**

SECTION ONE – FINGERBOARD KNOWLEDGE

The examiner may ask you to play *from memory* any of the scales, arpeggios or chords shown below. Scales and arpeggios should be played ascending and descending, i.e. from the lowest note to the highest and back again, without a pause and without repeating the top note. Chords should be played ascending only, and sounded string by string, starting with the lowest (root) note. To achieve a legato (i.e. smooth and over-ringing) sound, the whole chord shape should be placed on the fingerboard before, and kept on during, playing. Chords and arpeggios should be played tirando, i.e. using free strokes.

To allow for flexibility in teaching approaches, the right and left hand recommended fingering suggestions given below are *not* compulsory and alternative systematic fingerings, that are musically effective, will be accepted. Suggested tempos are for general guidance only. Slightly slower or faster performances will be acceptable, providing that the tempo is maintained evenly throughout.

Overall, the examiner will be listening for accurate, even and clear playing. Pressing with the tips of the left-hand fingers, as close to the fretwire as possible, will aid clarity.

A maximum of 15 marks may be awarded in this section of the examination.

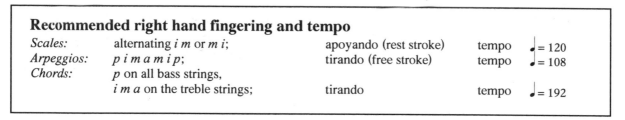

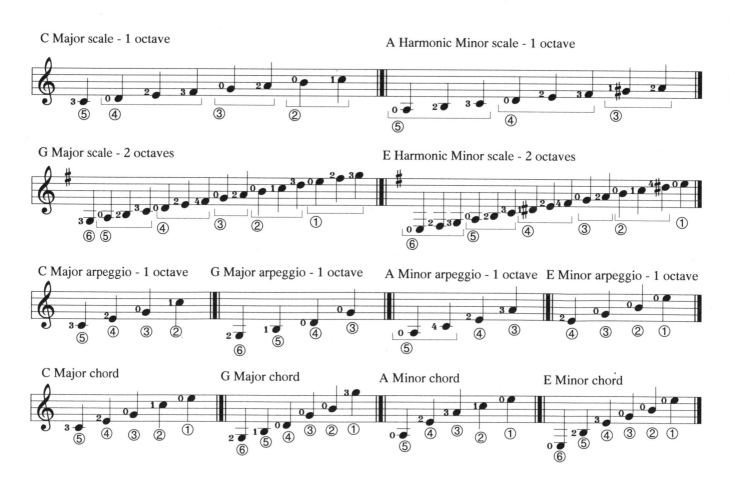

4

SECTION TWO – PERFORMANCE

Candidates should play *one* piece from *each* of the three groups. A maximum of 60 marks may be awarded in this section of the examination – i.e. up to 20 marks for each performance. Fingering and tempo markings are for general guidance only and do not need to be adhered to strictly. All repeat markings should be followed.

Performance Tips

Melodies:

The first three melodies are all in the key of G major, with the *Swan Lake* theme being in the key of E minor. Consequently, apart from some accidentals which may appear, the notes contained in the melodies are taken mainly from the G major or E harmonic minor scale shown in Section One of this handbook. Revision of these scales would provide helpful preparation before studying the melodies.

Ensure that you identify, and bring out, the *phrasing* within each melody. The examiner will be listening for the demonstration of structured melodic shaping within each performance.

Andante:

This piece, in $\frac{3}{4}$ time, is in the key of C major. Although often written as single notes, the piece features the C major chord quite regularly; so, wherever possible, keep your fingers on to form the chord. Examples of this can be seen in bars 1 and 2, and in bars 15 and 16, where all the notes comprise a C major chord.

Allegretto:

This piece in $\frac{2}{4}$ time is essentially in the key of C major. It is important that the bass notes, which are mainly minims, are held for their full value whilst the treble notes are played. In bars 5 and 21, playing the note of C with the second finger enables a smooth change to the low F note that opens the following bar.

Andantino:

This piece in $\frac{2}{4}$ time is essentially in the key of C major, with the first bar based on a partial C major chord. The repeated open G string note should not be played too loudly, as this would distract from the melody. You could even omit the repeated G note when practising the piece at first.

Ecossaise:

This piece in $\frac{2}{4}$ time is essentially in the key of A minor. The title means 'Scottish/Country Dance'. The words *D.C. al Fine,* that appear at the end of the piece, indicate that it should be played again from the beginning and should end after bar 8.

Greensleeves:

This piece in $\frac{3}{4}$ time is essentially in the key of A minor. The piece features a *dotted rhythm* in many bars, which adds a sense of movement and lilt to the piece. Care needs to be taken to observe rhythmic changes, such as between bars 12 and 13 – where one bar is dotted and the following bar is straight.

Gigue:

This piece in $\frac{3}{4}$ time is in the key of C major. It is important that the lower voice notes are sustained for their full value and care needs to be taken that these are not cut short. As with *Greensleeves*, the piece features a *dotted rhythm* in many bars.

Laika The Space Dog:

This piece in $\frac{4}{4}$ time is in the key of E minor. The melody is in the bass, so play these notes louder and hold them for their full value. Adjust the dynamics gently to create a floating spacey feel – especially in the middle section. The composer describes his inspiration for the piece as follows: "Early scientific research on the effects of space flight was done on animals. A dog named Laika was blasted into orbit, with no provision to bring her safely back to earth".

Scared Of The Dark:

This piece in $\frac{4}{4}$ time is in the key of E minor. To capture the mood of the piece, the tempo must be well controlled and the dynamic markings accurately followed. The notes marked with an accent sign (>) should be played strongly using a rest stroke. Each of these notes should be played after the 4th crotchet in the bass, and allowed to ring on until the next accented note occurs. In bars 10 to 13, each treble note should be played directly after each E bass note, giving a 1&2&3&4& effect. The repetitious left-hand fingering in these bars is designed to give a continuity of tone.

Sheep May Safely Graze

Johann Sebastian Bach
(1685 - 1750)

[Group A]

Ninth Symphony Theme (Ode To Joy)

Ludwig van Beethoven
(1770 - 1827)

[Group A]

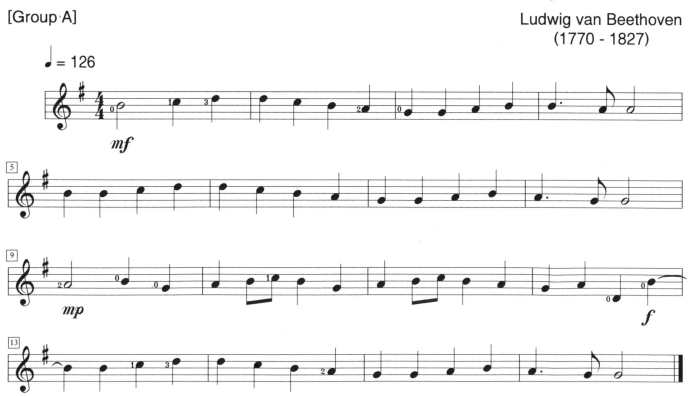

Lullaby Op.49 No.4

Johannes Brahms
(1833 - 1897)

[Group A]

♩ = 84

No.1 Scène from Swan Lake

Peter Ilyich Tchaikovsky
(1840 - 1893)

[Group A]

♩ = 88

7

Andante Op.31 No.1

[Group B]

Fernando Sor
(1778 - 1839)

Allegretto Op.39 No.4

[Group B]

Anton Diabelli
(1781-1858)

Andantino from Op.59

[Group B]

Matteo Carcassi
(1792-1853)

9

Ecossaise Op.33 No.10

Mauro Giuliani
(1781-1829)

[Group B]

Greensleeves

Anonymous
(16th Century)

[Group C]

Gigue

[Group C]

Johann Anton Logy
(1650 - 1721)

Laika The Space Dog

[Group C]

Marc Catley
(1959 -)

Scared Of The Dark

[Group C]

Tony Skinner
(1960 -)

SECTION THREE – MUSICAL KNOWLEDGE

A maximum of 7 marks may be awarded in this section of the examination. The examiner will ask questions, based on the music performed, to test the candidate's knowledge of the treble clef and stave, bar lines, notes and rests, key and time signatures, accidentals, basic musical terms and signs. The information below provides a summary of what is required.

The clef and stave

The notes on the lines (E G B D F) can be remembered by making up an unusual phrase such as: <u>E</u>normous <u>G</u>uitarists <u>B</u>reak <u>D</u>ainty <u>F</u>ootstools.

The notes in the spaces between the lines form the word FACE.

The treble clef is also known as the *G clef* – since it is drawn looped around the G line.

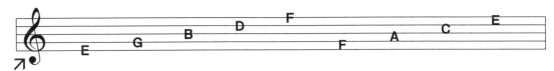

Treble Clef

Bar lines

A bar is a way of dividing music into manageable portions. It makes music easier to read and makes it easier to discover where the main beat lies. The end of each bar is indicated by a vertical line called a bar line. The space between each pair of bar lines, where the notes are written, is called a bar (or measure). At the end of a piece, or section, of music there are two vertical lines; these are called a *double bar line*.

Notes and rests

The table below shows the names of the notes and rests, and their values.

Traditional name	Modern name	Note	Rest	Value in crotchet beats
semibreve	whole note	o	▬	4
dotted minim	dotted half note	♩.	▬ .	3
minim	half note	♩	▬	2
dotted crotchet	dotted quarter note	♩.	𝄽 ·	1½
crotchet	quarter note	♩	𝄽	1
quaver	eighth note	♪	♩	½

Dots and ties

A dot after a note increases the value of that note by half of its original value. For example, a dotted crotchet is equivalent to 3 quavers in length, whereas a normal crotchet is equivalent to 2 quavers in length. A second dot after a note increases the value of that note by half of the value of the first dot. For example, a double dotted minim is equivalent in length to 7 quavers (i.e. 4 for the main minim, 2 for the first dot, and 1 for the second dot).

The value of a note may also be increased by the use of a tie: only the first note is played, but it is held on for its own length plus that of the following tied note. The tied note in the example below lasts for the equivalent of 3 quavers.

dotted crotchet   double dotted minim   tie

Key signature

C Major or A Minor   G Major or E Minor

Where there is one sharp at the beginning of each stave of a piece of music, this indicates that the key is either G major or E minor. Where one sharp occurs it will always be on the top F line, and indicates that all F notes should be played as F#. Where there is no visible key signature the key will be C major or A minor.

A sharp, flat or natural that appears during a piece of music, rather than as part of the key signature, is called an *accidental*. It has the effect of sharpening or flattening just that one note, and any others at the same pitch within the same bar. It does not affect notes in the remaining bars, as bar lines cancel all accidentals.

Time signature

The numbers that appear at the beginning of a piece of music are called the time signature. The top number shows the number of beats per bar, whilst the bottom number indicates the value of each beat. For example, ⁴₄ means four crotchet beats (i.e. four quarter notes) per bar.

Terms and signs

Candidates should be able to identify any basic terms and signs that appear in the music performed. Some examples are given below.

> accent

Rall. (rallentando)   becoming gradually slower

Rit. (ritenuto)   held back

a tempo   in time, i.e. return to previous speed

D. C. al Fine   repeat from the beginning up to the point marked *Fine* (the end)

♩ = 120   metronome tempo

Repeat sign.
(Play from the previous 2 vertical dots, or, in their absence, from the beginning.)

Dynamics

pp	*p*	*mp*	*mf*	*f*	*ff*
pianissimo	*piano*	*mezzo-piano*	*mezzo-forte*	*forte*	*fortissimo*
very soft	soft	medium soft	medium loud	loud	very loud

crescendo – getting louder

decrescendo / diminuendo – getting softer

SECTION FOUR – PLAYING AT SIGHT

The examiner will show you the sight reading test and allow you just a short time to look over it before performing it. A maximum of 10 marks may be awarded in this section of the examination. The table below shows the range of the piece:

Length	Keys	Time signatures	Note values	Fingerboard positions
4 bars	Major: C, G Minor: A, E	2 3 4 4	♩ ♩ ♫	1st

PERFORMANCE TIPS

1. Always check the key and time signature BEFORE you start to play.

2. Once you have identified the key it is helpful to remember that the notes will all come from the key scale – which you should already know from Section One of this handbook. This means that it will generally be easier to play the sight reading if you use the same fingering as you have used for playing the scale.

3. Before you start to play, quickly scan through the piece and check any notes or rhythms that you are unsure of.

4. Note the tempo or style marking, but be careful not to play at a tempo at which you cannot maintain accuracy throughout.

5. Once you start to play, try and keep your eyes on the music. Avoid the temptation to keep looking at the fingerboard – that's a sure way to lose your place in the music.

6. If you do make an error, try not to let it affect your confidence for the rest of the piece. It is better to keep going and capture the overall shape of the piece, rather than stopping and going back to correct errors.

The following examples show the *type* of pieces that will be presented in the examination.

(i) Moderato

(ii) Andante

(iii) Moderato

(iv) Andante

(v) Moderato

(vi) Adagio

(vii) Moderato

(viii) Allegretto

SECTION FIVE – AURAL AWARENESS

A maximum of 8 marks may be awarded in this section of the examination – i.e. up to 2 marks per test. The tests will be played by the examiner on either guitar or piano, at the examiner's discretion. The examples below are shown in guitar notation and give a broad indication of the type of tests that will be given during the examination. Candidates wishing to view the piano notation for these tests should obtain the London College Of Music *Sample Ear Tests* booklet.

Rhythm tests

1. After the examiner has played a short piece of music, similar to one of the examples below, the candidate will be asked to identify the time signature as *2* or *3* time.

2. The examiner will play the piece again and the candidate should clap or tap along in time on each pulse beat, accenting the first beat of each bar.

Pitch tests

1. The examiner will play two notes consecutively, similar to the examples below. The candidate will be asked to identify, as "first" or "second", which one was the lower or higher note. The candidate will then be asked to sing the lower or higher of the two notes as requested by the examiner. The examiner may conduct this test twice, using a different pair of notes during the second test.

2. The examiner will play a short melody in a major key, but will not play the final closing note. The candidate should sing the missing final note, which will be the tonic note of the key. (The examiner will select a suitable key and octave according to the gender and age of the candidate.) The tonic chord will be sounded first.

London College of **Music & Media**
THAMES VALLEY UNIVERSITY

Examination Entry Form
for
Classical Guitar

GRADE ONE
or Leisure Play Preliminary

PLEASE COMPLETE CLEARLY IN INK AND IN BLOCK CAPITAL LETTERS

SESSION (Spring/Summer/Winter): _____ YEAR: _____

Preferred Examination Centre (if known): _____
If left blank you will examined at the nearest venue to your home address.

Candidate Details:

Candidate Name (as to appear on certificate):

_____

Address: _____

_____ Postcode: _____

Tel. No. (day): _____ (evening): _____

Tick this box if you are also entering for LCM Theory of Music ☐
If so, which Grade? _____

Teacher Details:

Teacher Name (as to appear on certificate): _____

LCM Teacher Code (if entered previously): _____

RGT Tutor Code (if applicable): _____

Address: _____

_____ Postcode: _____

Tel. No. (day): _____ (evening): _____

Tick this box if any details above have changed since your last LCM entry ☐

Tick this box if the teacher has also entered pupils for ☐
RGT Electric or Bass Guitar examinations for the same session.

IMPORTANT NOTES

- It is the candidate's responsibility to have knowledge of, and comply with, the current syllabus requirements. Where candidates are entered for examinations by a teacher, the teacher must take responsibility that candidates are entered in accordance with the current syllabus requirements. Failure to carry out any of the examination requirements may lead to disqualification.
- For candidates with special needs, a letter giving details, and medical certificate as appropriate, should be attached.
- Any practical appointment requests (e.g. 'prefer morning,' or 'prefer weekdays') must be made at the time of entry. **LCM and its Representatives will take note of the information given, however, no guarantees can be made that all wishes will be met.**
- Submission of this entry is an undertaking to abide by the current regulations as listed in the current syllabus and any subsequent regulations updates published in the LCM Examinations Newsletter issued each term.
- Entries for public centres should be sent **to the LCM local representative**. Contact the LCM office for details of your nearest centre or to enquire about setting up your own centre.

Examination Fee   £ _____

Late Entry Fee (if necessary)   £ _____

Total amount submitted   £ _____
Cheques or postal orders should be made payable to **'Thames Valley University'**.

A current list of fees and entry deadlines is available from LCM Exams.

LCM Exams
Thames Valley University
St Mary's Road
London
W5 5RF

Tel: 020 8231 2364
Fax: 020 8231 2433

e-mail: lcm.exams@tvu.ac.uk

The standard LCM music entry form is NOT valid for Classical Guitar entries. **Entry to the examination is only possible via this original form. Photocopies of this form will not be accepted under any circumstances.**

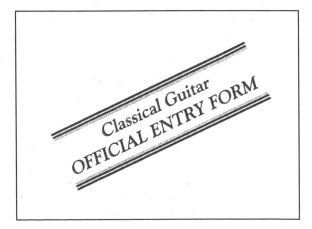